The Garden of My Heart

# The Garden of My Heart

### Donna Tipton Howell

# *Acknowledgments*

Special thanks to Jason Leber and
N.D. Greenman who helped with all
the unknowns of putting my blog posts
and poems together in book form.
Also, thanks to my husband, family,
Ladies Bible Class and church friends
who listen patiently when I want to share my
pieces. They are my inspiration!

# Contents

# *Introduction*

    I've never considered myself to be an author, but I have enjoyed teaching writing to my students, from elementary through college age, and have always written along with my students so I could share models of different genres.  Writing is a way of comforting myself when some sort of emotion is inside that needs to find a way out.  After retiring I needed to still write some so I started a blog called "Sharings of the Sisterhood."  My sister, Kelly, and some of my family members contributed as well. This book is composed of some of my own writings for the blog, and poems I have written over the years.  The marriage poem sprang from a study with my Ladies Bible Class I was teaching.  I asked for advice from church friends that they might give to newlyweds, and then I used that advice in writing a "Recipe for Marriage." A few years back I tried to find my writings to put them together, and they were scattered here and there, so I decided to keep them together, along with some of my photos, here in this book.  Writing is a very personal experience and I tried to encourage my students to share their work so that others will see the comfort and healing that personal writing can bring.  Everyone is a writer.  If you can think and talk, just write it on paper and you are a writer!

*Donna Tipton Howell*

# Granny's House

My mind wonders back on all those years
And there's one place it often goes
It's Granny's house, my special place
And all who've been there know

A kind of magic is in that house
For years I have tried to figure
Just what it was that made it so
And some reasons I'd consider

Maybe it was the aroma
Of dumplings and fried apple pie
And the feasts that were spread on the table
For those who might happen by

Or could it have been all the noises
Of laughter that rang in my ear
Or the still quiet sounds of silence
As we bowed our heads in prayer

And then I considered the feelings
That being with family bears
The comfort and the security
Of being with someone who cares

Could it be that the house that she lived in
Gives off comfort and warmth by itself?
If I could build one just like it
Forever, I'd live in that wealth!

And so, I determined to build it
I drew up a plan in my heart
A two story brick with a welcoming gate
Would give me a good place to start

I'd need some flowers and bushes
I hope they aren't too hard to find
Like lilacs and lilies and clover
That heady and sweet-smelling kind

And it has to have plenty of porches
For sitting and rocking and such
And a sidewalk that's marked to play hopscotch
And a feather bed soft to the touch

And so, I continued my planning
In hopes that it wouldn't be long
Till I'd be in a house just like Granny's
And change into right what was wrong

But then, as I stopped to remember
All the wonderful times in that place
It came to me all in a moment
When I thought of her beautiful face

It wasn't her house that was special
Or a potion that was sprinkled there
The magic was all in a person
It was because my Granny was there

So, I won't build a house just like Granny's
Or wait for the magic to start
I'll just strive to become so much like her
So the magic will live in my heart

# The Garden of Our Hearts

It's Springtime in Kentucky. The flower garden is soft with last night's rain still glistening on the tiny sprigs of new growth that will soon shoot up into full grown weeds. The earth will harden with long hours of warm sun, and the roots will spread deep into the soil. If I wait 'til then, I will try pulling the weed out, but it will snap off at ground level, leaving the roots embedded to spring back, doubling or tripling the plant's height.

I thought of this when I decided to pull a few little tiny sprouts from the flower bed. The tender young plant can be carefully pinched at the bottom of the stem and the top of the root, and gently wiggled, and slowly pulled from the soil, root and all. This is a good feeling to get the whole root in one careful pull. As I pulled them out, one by one, I thought of the Scriptures and of terms used by Jesus and the apostles that speak to this act of weeding out the dark parts of ourselves that need to be fully plucked out.

Those roots, such as envy, anger, greed, impatience, lust, whatever the sin, if left in my heart, will become so twisted and entwined into my being that it may eventually become too hard to pluck out of my life, leaving me rooted in bitterness. *"Strive for peace with everyone, and for the holiness, without which, no one will see the Lord. See to it that no one fails to obtain the grace of God; that no 'root of bitterness' springs up and causes trouble, and by it many become defiled"* (Heb. 12:14-15, ESV).

So where do I begin? First, I have to recognize the weeds from the flowers. Sometimes I rush ahead, without taking time to make sure. Going to the plant guide is the best way to determine an unknown. And in our lives, going to the Scripture, which is written by our Maker, is the best way to learn what needs to be plucked out. And our conscience, if correctly trained also helps us know the weeds from the flowers.

Gardeners who become experts will testify it takes careful study and following of directions to grow the best flowers. But it also requires discipline. It is easy to forget the tiny sprigs in the spring that look so small and innocent. Yet in only a little while, if left untended, they grow into huge, ugly weeds that take over the whole garden, leaving little room for the pretty blooming flowers for which the garden was meant. And whether we acknowledge Him or not, it takes sunshine and rain from God to make the flowers grow.

Getting to the root of the problem is not easy. A careful and prayerful search inside our own inner being takes effort, study, discipline, and courage. Plucking it out is often painful, as we must humble ourselves and acknowledge our own sinfulness and need for God's help. But it is such a good feeling to fully pull it out from the root, and tossing it away, knowing that your heart is now clean and ready to grow something good.

So plant a garden with your children. And while they are pulling the tiny weed sprouts and planting the tiny seeds, teach them about how God wants us to take all the bad things (like lying, selfishness, etc.) out of our lives and plant happy, pretty things (like truthfulness, and sharing) into our hearts, so we can grow a beautiful garden of flowers in our hearts. And thank Him for the sunshine and rain, and all the spiritual blessings sent to those who love Him.

# Highway of Life

We're traveling the road, called the Highway of Life
It's full speed ahead! Past triumphs and strife
We manage to deal with these detours, it seems
With barely a waiver from daily routines

But sometimes, alas, we're stunned to discover,
That it's time to slow down...or even, pull over
Life seems quite different from this vantage view
And it's there we discover what really is true

We're pulled over usually by chance, and not choice
And we try to protest, but inside some voice...
Is whispering, "Be still, and give this a chance"
So you give life a stare, instead of a glance

What you see is a boy, whose smile makes you melt
In the fast lane of life, you forgot how that felt
You smell the sweet breath of the one you are rocking
While the birds through the window are singing and mocking

It could be that tragedy, sickness or grief
Has you off of life's road and you're seeking relief
When suddenly the kindness and sweetness of others
Is just what you need, and you start to recover

The lessons in life are often not found
In the fast, busy pace as we're rushing around
And in times when we think life is passing us by
It might be just then that we truly can fly

Upward we're climbing to that higher plane
Where there's goodness and patience, and maybe some pain
Where humility, meekness and compassion abound
And life's hidden treasures of love may be found

# A Brighter Shade of "The Blues"

The lady of the house is often the one who sets the mood for others, and so the old saying, "If Mama isn't happy, no one is happy" is often oh-so-true.

No matter how hard I resist, sometimes I just get a case of "The Blues." It seems to be genetic to some degree. My sweet mother battled severe depression and anxiety most of her life, and I stood by often with a feeling of utter helplessness. Though some cases like hers were so extreme no cure was found, for most of us, we can learn ways to help us through this dark part of our lives. Here are a few tips that have helped me find a bit brighter shade of "The Blues."

• **Recognize early on when you begin feeling down.** Getting hold of the situation before you fall too low to climb up is always a plus.

• **Notice changes that may be associated with these blue episodes.** Hormones, lack of sleep, stress, may be helping these blues along. Try and adjust as much as possible. For hormones, talk with your doctor and other women for ideas.

• **Walk!** It sounds too simple, but often a good brisk walk will help lift those endorphins and lift your spirits as well. Other exercise works too. And I am one of those who really need actual sunshine to come down on me, so I get outside in the sun whenever I can.

• **Realize others around you are not to blame.** A tendency is to think others are bringing you down by what they do or say, but that will not help, even if it is partly true. You must look inside your own negative thoughts and try and change your own outlook, rather than focusing on wrongs done unto you by others.

• **Act!** Get up. Get out. Get going! Find someone who is even lower than you and give them a visit. It has helped me many times to force myself to go and see someone who needs a visit, just to find out upon leaving, that I gained more than I gave.

• **Pray.** This should probably be first on the list. Isn't it interesting that whatever we are trying to work on in our lives, we always need to be praying? Yet, when I have "The Blues," it is hard to get out of my own self enough to even think to pray. And when I do pray, I often try and analyze and fix everything, rather than really turning it over fully to God.

• **Read and meditate.** When my blues last longer than a couple of hours, and move into a couple of days, I have noticed that most often my Bible reading efforts have slacked off, along with my prayers.

Sometimes just getting God's word flowing back in my thoughts is enough to lift my mood. Even if it is one or two verses that I can stop and really apply to my own life, it begins renewing and refreshing me.

• **Laugh.** It seems when I get down, I can bring others right on down with me. Often letting go and having a good laugh at something funny, or even at myself, will aid in lifting that heavy heart.

• **Cry hard and talk it out!** And sometimes, if something outside of you is going on that is keeping you from rising from your blues, you may just have to tell someone and have a good cry. Keeping too much inside is often harmful. Knowing when to let things pass and when you really need to talk it out is quite difficult, so try and keep this to a minimum, but when it has to be done, just do it.

• **Go to EVERY church service.** It may be a temptation to skip the assembly of the saints when you are down. I can't emphasize this enough. Do not miss! This is where you will get the most refreshment! This is your best place to get to a brighter place in yourself.

• **Hope.** And last of all, keep your hope alive. I've always tried to have something to look forward to. Whether it be going out to eat on a Friday night, or going to a tag sale to buy something for my store. But mostly, my hope in Christ is what remains my anchor. He holds my soul in the grasp of His hand, leads me through my dark blues, and reminds me of a heavenly sunlight that awaits me if I remain faithful to Him. A sunlight that will always shine down on me, and where every shade of blue will be bright and pure and lovely.

# The Hidden Part

Sometimes when life feels empty
And I don't know where to start
I wonder if the clues I need
Are locked up in my heart

I try to look inside myself
To see what I'm about
To satisfy the longings
From inside and without

And then I might remember
There are tools that I might use
To find what's hidden in myself
And to understand the clues

So I gather first my flashlight
I illuminate my mind
It is, of course, the Bible
Filled with treasures for to find

I shine it on my inward self
And look into the mirror
I see the things I've left undone
"Be a doer, not a hearer"

And now I say unto myself
Look closer if you dare
and I find another empty hole
It's the time not spent in prayer

Oh yes, I know I'm busy
With much in disarray
There doesn't seem to be much time
To study and to pray

So I open up the word of God
And I find the hidden part
Eternity is deep inside
God placed it in my heart

So that is what those longings are!
That seem to haunt me so
I must start to treasure things above
For my eternal self to grow

I'll take my worries to the Rock
I'll talk to Him in prayer
I'll sing praises to His mighty name
His glories I'll declare

Now finally those empty holes
Are starting to be filled
And all my cares and anxious thoughts
Are starting to be stilled

I want to learn to trust Him
In everything I do
I want to give Him all myself
For His promises are true

I thank you God for answering
With mercy and with love
The questions of this earthly life
With answers from above

And thank you for your patience
That you show me every day
And guiding me to choose the path
The truth, the life, the way

# Five Tips for Satisfying Worship

You have probably heard, and may have even thought, "I didn't get much out of the service today." Perhaps looking from a new perspective might eliminate that sentiment. Here are a few tips for refreshing your mind and spirit in service to the Lord.

**1. Prepare** – One of my recurring nightmares is going into the school classroom and realizing I haven't prepared fully for the day. When I mentored new teachers, the first thing I stressed was having a plan. You will get very little from a service if you don't get your mind and heart ready to worship. Pray for the service before you leave your home. Pray for the teachers, the song leaders, individual members. Study your lesson. I love to read the lesson right before leaving to have it fresh on my mind. If you have a lesson book, answer all the questions.

**2. Participate** – Find a way to contribute. Arrive early and greet everyone with a hug and a smile. Ask about their family, their health, their life. Really listen to others. You will soon find you are anxious to see one another and anxious for the next gathering. Philippians 4:21, *"Greet every saint in Christ Jesus"* (ESV). Can you teach a class? Can you assist someone else who is teaching? Can you contribute to the class discussion? Can you prepare the communion? Can you be the best listener in the house during the sermon? Can you encourage the preacher by telling him how much you appreciate his devotion to study so that you can learn new and exciting things every week about God's word? Can you listen interactively, applying each new point to some area of your own life? Psalm 95:6-7 says, *"Oh come let us worship and bow down; let us kneel before the Lord, our Maker! For He is our God, and we are the people of his pasture, and the sheep of his hand"* (ESV).

**3. Mentor** – Choose someone a bit younger than you, or newer to the faith. Put real energy into developing a relationship. Offer suggestions of things you learned that helped you. Is it a mom with a new baby? Offer assistance. Encourage. Tell her how much you appreciate her efforts in raising her children in the Lord. Is there a teenager you can get to know? Ask about school. Learn about his/her interests. Go watch her in a chorus concert or a soccer game. Is there a widow who is learning to cope without her spouse? Sit beside her. Listen to her and let her know you love her. Is there a child who is just learning to read? Show them the words in the song book. Get down on your knees and listen as he tells you about his day. Hug him and tell him you love him. You will look up one day and find the one you mentored in the past is now your best encourager!

**4. Love** – Everyone can do this, but it is not as easy as it may sound. Once again, I return to my Dad's definition of love as "a stern devotion to duty." This means that if we devote ourselves to the task, we can learn to love those not-so-easy-to-love folks too! Again, it means forgetting self and showing a genuine interest in others. This takes time, but like the slow drip of water on the rocks, over time it will carve a river of love that can feed a once-thirsty soul. And most of all, learn to love God for His amazing plan from the beginning of time to make us His children. And to love Christ, who gave Himself for our sins and died so that we might have life!

**5. Be Passionate!!!** – This is my favorite one! When my principal told me he wanted me to teach 4th grade science I warned him that was not my expertise. But he had confidence in me and so I decided to become passionate about each new lesson. I would try and come up with a way to make it exciting to the kids, and I actually ended up enjoying the lessons myself. Now as I teach the preschool and primary class on Wednesday nights at church, I try and learn as much as I can about the lesson for my own growth, and it is easy to become passionate about God's word as I see how it changes my life. I try and transfer this passion to the children. If you teach, do it with passion. If you sing, put your whole heart into the song. Singing with passion to God and to your brethren. Psalm 95:1 says, *"Oh come, let us sing to the Lord; let us make a joyful noise to the rock of our salvation!"* (ESV) Be passionate about the prayers, becoming wholly involved as you pray along silently with the leader. Be passionate about the people who are trying to live for Jesus and are helping you along.

All the above tips focus on doing…giving…sharing…and serving. They do not consider receiving…getting…or being served. And when we have practiced these things, God's words will ring true in our ears, reminding us that *"It is more blessed to give than to receive"* (Acts 20:35, ESV). And we will go away refreshed and satisfied from every single service we attend.

# My Front Porch

Some wood and wicker rocking chairs
A swing on either end
Oft they're filled with family
neighbors and good friends

It may be rain or sunshine
If the temperature is right
And even if a bit too-cool
Just tuck a blanket tight

Some flowers blooming in the front
Help set the country scene
A fresh mown lawn, the lofty trees
All different shades of green

The porch can also be a place
To wile the time away
To give thanks for all the Lord has done
To look to Him and pray

Sometimes I watch the chipmunks
And listen to the birds
And contemplate the beauty
Of God's amazing world

I've sat on this old porch swing
To reminisce the day
Held babies in the rocking chair
And watched the children play

Badminton in the front yard
Croquet and wiffle ball
Some horseshoe and some corn-hole
For children big and small

Cartwheels in the yard
As it began to rain
And fireflies in a jar
To let them go again

The front porch is a good place
To watch them rake the hay
And load it on the wagon
On a hot and steamy day

The porch has hosted potlucks
And singing song refrains
And celebrating birthdays
And weddings in the rain

The front steps serve as risers
For photographs of groups
At Christmas and Thanksgiving
And celebrations too

When we got our little puppy
We brought him to that place
While each child hugged and welcomed him
He licked them on the face

We've rocked and read our Bibles
And had some great debates
Our kids had lots of questions
We've talked till it was late

Games and trivia battles
Politics and sports
We laughed together often
And developed a rapport

And even though the kids have gone
Their own and separate ways
Still when they come to visit us
They know I'm going to say

Who wants to go and sit with me
Let's go out the front door
Let's rock and share some memories
And then we'll make some more

So why not come and sit awhile
And have a glass of tea
We'll knit some on our tie-that-binds
And make YOU some memories

# Too Busy
## (I Want to Be a Christian, But...)

I want to be a Christian
And I'll go to church sometimes
Especially Sunday morning
And maybe Sunday nights

But don't look for me on Wednesday
I'm tired from work by then
And maybe in a meeting
I'll show up when I can

I want to go to heaven
When this dear life is done
But now I can't be bothered much
Even now I have to run

I have to do my yard work
And the house is such a mess
And Susie has a game tonight
And I really need some rest

I hope you have a big crowd
Of folks with less to do
It's good to know the work goes on
I'll pray for all of you

When I was in my 20's
Between college and career
I didn't get to church much
But I planned to go "next year"

Then I moved into my 30's
With a house and job and wife
I meant to go to church more
But it was such a crazy life!

Now I've just turned 40
And the Lord should understand
That I have my obligations
But I'll get there when I can

Even though I want to worship
I have no time to spare
As soon as all the kids leave home
I promise I'll be there

You really should be thankful
That I get there when I do
I think I've sacrificed a lot
To come and worship You

I just have one more question
Before I leave you now
It's how to get my kids to come
When I get to church somehow

I get up Sunday mornings
And say "It's time to run!"
But they say "I have a headache"
Or "I have homework to be done"

I don't know what has happened
To make them act this way
I hope you have the answer
Of what I might can say

I don't know why they make excuse
To stay home on Sunday morning
My wife and I have taught them well
This happened without warning

I'll talk with you about this
At some later date and time
You know I have so much to do
And it will work out fine

I know when I get older
There won't be much to do
So right now, let me do my stuff
I'll see you when I'm through

# Recipe for Marriage

## Ingredients & Directions

Preheat with fervent love for God
Start with 1 man and 1 woman with 2 heaping cups of love for each other
and 2 hearts devoted to God
Mix together well
Add 1 lifetime commitment
Stir in submission, respect, truthfulness, and honor
Adding a dash of truth
Shake that all together till well blended
Gently fold in an ounce of forgiveness
Keep mixing above ingredients day by day
Open up a two-way line of communication
And use it often
Sprinkle in one part each:
Appreciation and
Thoughtfulness and
A daily dose of gentle and kind words
Carefully sift out any angry thoughts and harsh words
And little things that don't matter
Add a little fun and a lot of laughter
And sprinkle all over with hugs
Keep mixing the above ingredients
And baste daily with prayer, study, and worship
Bake continually in God's love
Enjoy for a lifetime

# Reconcilable Differences

I'm remembering a unit I taught to middle school students that I titled "Celebrating Our Differences." It was one of my favorite units and a student favorite as well. I would begin by having the whole class brainstorm, and then listing on the board all the ways we could think of that someone might use to tease or put down another. The students easily came up with tons of physical traits, like a person's height (too tall, too short), weight (fatty, beanpole), skin color, hair, eye sight (wearing glasses, blind), complexion (freckles, pimples, birth marks); social traits included economic status, friends, groups, family, where you live, clubs, parents jobs, etc.; and there were behavioral traits like shyness or blushing, or too loud, obnoxious, too silly, too quiet, too serious; finally we included mental abilities such as "too smart" or "not smart enough" or bad grades or grades that made you the teacher's pet and on and on.

It was amazing how long a list the students could generate in just a few minutes. Then we would discuss how it feels to be teased, and why someone would want to hurt another. Occasionally I would get a student who claimed to never have been teased, but really everyone could identify with this lesson in one way or another. So from that we would springboard into what life might be like if there were no

28

differences. We decided that would not be good and that differences make life spicy and exciting. Our differences provide us with those who can entertain us, teach us new things, and inspire us to be better. Students went on to write some of the best pieces I ever read over my teaching years. They wrote poems, personal essays, fiction, all with the same theme of celebrating our differences rather than allowing them to be a vehicle for harm.

Still, though each student fully understood the implications of teasing due to differences, invariably, not long after the lesson, I would find myself dealing with issues of students hurting each other deeply by teasings and put-downs. It seems our carnal nature deceives us into thinking that by putting someone else down, it will make us look better. What it actually does is to lower us in the eyes of others, and in our own self-worth as well. As parents we spend lots of time and energy teaching our children about the golden rule and treating others (usually beginning with siblings and then peers) as we would like to be treated, and not judging others by outward appearance. However, we often find ourselves guilty of these same injustices in our own relationships.

When I was young rarely did anyone use the word "divorce" and it was a great scandal, usually due to adultery on one partner, when it did occur. Then came the concept of divorce due to "irreconcilable differences." Wow! What a new concept! People are different! The person you marry is not exactly like you! So when a couple falls in love, the differences are celebrated. One likes to travel, the other does not. One loves sports, the other can take it or leave it. One loves to spend time hiking outdoors, the other likes to be inside. How are these differences reconciled? Well, if you think back, you so wanted to please each other, and just being together was such a delight, you found ways to do what the other person liked, and you actually found yourself enjoying it! How refreshing to share a relationship with someone who can step out of his or her own comfort zone and see from another perspective.

Unfortunately, in many marriages, it turns into, "Well, that's not really something I want to do right now" or "Why won't you ever do what I want?" instead of "Sure, let's try it?" or "That sounds interesting." We often step back into our own small little world and refuse to entertain any idea of a different way of thinking or doing something. Before long we hear those words "irreconcilable differences," solely because we chose not to reconcile our differences and celebrate the uniqueness we each bring to our marriage relationship.

What are we teaching our children when we pout and sulk because we don't get our way? And on the other hand, what wonderful lessons can we show them when we anxiously accept a new challenge to try something different with the one who is given to us to as our life-companion? Should it startle us to read what God instructed to make a happy marriage? Wives are to *submit to your own husbands as to the Lord*…and husbands are to *love your wives as Christ loved the church* and love her as if she is you own body for *no one ever hated his own flesh, but nourishes and cherishes it* (Eph. 5:22-31, ESV). In just a few sentences He gives us the means by which we can reconcile all our differences, and that is by submitting to each other's wishes as much as possible. So let us spice up our lives, and step out of our tiny world, by celebrating that we have differences and learning to reconcile ourselves to the one we vowed to love, honor and cherish, and till death do us part.

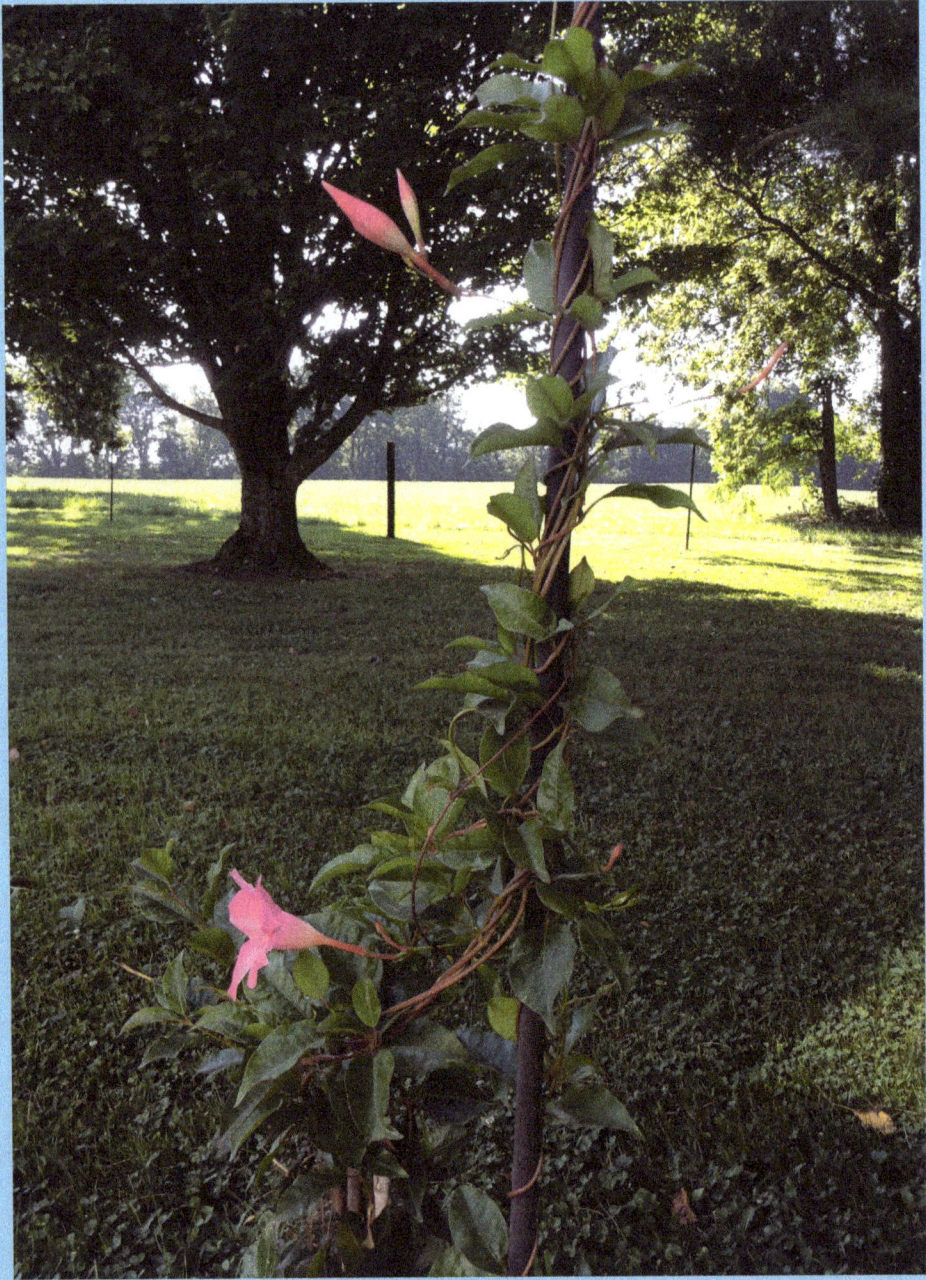

# Tiny Raindrop

A tiny little raindrop fell
And after it another
Which didn't make much impact
In the hard and rocky cover

But they started a consistent drip
Onto that stony ground
The water trickled in a path
A stream could now be found

And after that more single drops
Would gather close together
And fall into the flowing stream
In rain and stormy weather

And so, the stream became so big
It turned into a river
What started as just single drops
Was much more when bound together

And like those drops we are alone
Until we join with others
For every time we get the chance
With sisters and our brothers

And we know that God is with us
If we're walking in His light
But He also gave us friends on earth
To help us win the fight

Each week we meet at worship time
We love to be together
We sing and study and we pray
And learn to love each other

And pretty soon the years go by
One drip behind another
And all at once a mighty bond
Has linked us all together

No more is each a single drop
To handle things alone
But now there is a family
Together we are one

We've joined ourselves with others
To face the storms that come
We'll hold each other's hands until
He comes to take us home

# Five Lessons I Learned from My Dad

1. **I learned to define love.** The definition of love, according to Dad: **"Love is stern devotion to duty."** In my teen years, when I first asked Dad about love, this is what he told me. I did not really like that definition at that time. My head gave this a quick review, but my heart did not want to embrace this idea. My dreams were bigger than that. There was really nothing appealing about that concept that such a lofty thing as LOVE should be explained in such a humble light. But, I kept that definition in my head, and as I watched Dad live out that love, it began to find its way into my heart as well. There really is no explanation needed. Just observe someone who is putting it into action, and you will likely find you've been converted to that definition just as I was. 1 Corinthians 13:4-8, *"Love…does not insist on its own way…Love bears all things, believes all things, hopes all things, endures all things. Love never ends"* (ESV).

2. **I learned to take a wrong.** There were times growing up when I even argued with Dad about standing up for what was rightfully his. Both in his business and personal relationships, I saw Dad give up his money, his time, and even his will, in order to keep the peace. Though he would not bend on what he believed the Holy Scriptures to teach, in every other walk of life he was willing to take a hit and move on. I'm still working on this one! 1 Peter 2:20, *"…But if, when you do good and suffer for*

*it you endure, this is a gracious thing in the sight of God"* (ESV).

3. **I learned the difference between "teaching" and "training."** Both terms are used in one of Dad's favorite passages: 2 Timothy 3:16, *"All Scripture is breathed out by God, and profitable for teaching, for reproof, for correction and for training in righteousness"* (ESV). Teaching must take place, but the glue that makes it stick is the **training**. The definition of **train**: *"to coach in, or accustom to a mode of behavior or performance; to make proficient with specialized instruction and practice"* (www.yourdictionary.com). I have a sign in my kitchen window that says, "Enjoy the little things, for one day you'll look back and realize they were the big things!" That has been true in so many ways. It's those little things, done almost without realizing, that make the biggest impact on who we become. These seemingly "little" things, practiced day by day, week by week, month by month, and year by year, eventually add up to something bigger than I can put into words. This is what keeps me on the path toward heaven: Prayer at every meal, attending every service of the church, giving liberally, studying God's word, practicing hospitality, talking about the Bible…practicing these consistently, without letting school, work, children's activities, or other interruptions interfere…this is what is meant by the writer in Proverbs 22:6, ***"Train up a child*** *in the way he should go; even when he is old he will not depart from it"* (ESV). And this is the training with which I was blessed.

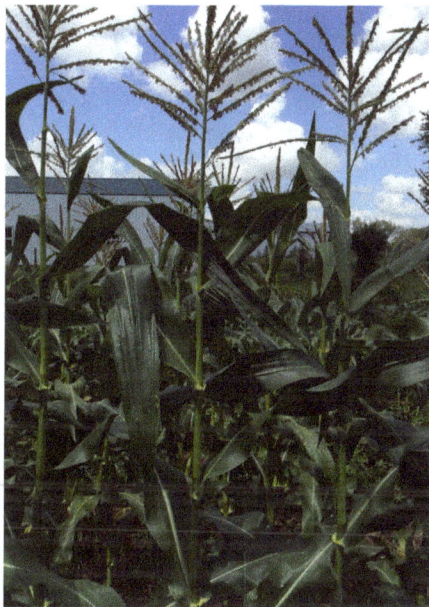

4. **I learned that things usually are better in the morning.** My dad witnessed many of my emotional meltdowns that would carry into the late evening hours. But he would say, "Go to bed. You can figure it out in the morning." I often remember that admonition when I feel as if nothing will work out, and time and again I make my plea (now to my heavenly father as I formerly did to Dad), I get into bed, and go to sleep, and when I awake his words have proven true. Matthew 6:25-31, *"Therefore I tell you, do not be anxious about your life…for you heavenly father knows what you need…but seek first the kingdom of God and His righteousness, and all things shall be added to you"* (ESV).

5. **I learned to work hard and finish what I start, no matter the cost.** If you start on the road to heaven, you will find many detours offered along life's journey. But as Dad said, stick to the strait and narrow road that leads to life. It is often the more difficult way, the unpopular way, the politically incorrect way, but it is the only way to life. That is what he lived, and so I will follow his steps and see him there one beautiful day. Matthew 7:14, *"For the gate is narrow and the way is hard that leads to life, and those who find it are few"* (ESV).

# Broken Heart

When your heart is broken
And you can feel the blues
If you would like to have some peace
There's something you can do

First get a cup of coffee
And look toward the sun
Or maybe take a walk outside
Or even take a run

You can sit and pat the dog
Or look out on the sea
Or maybe even write a list
Of good things that come free

You can give a helping hand
Or sew or make a cake
And if some leaves are on the ground
You might even grab a rake

These things can all contribute
To helping get you through
But I suggest you talk to God
And ask what He would do

For if you really trust Him
In good times and the bad
He really has the answers
And knows why you are sad

He'll make you look outside yourself
He'll help you see the light
But first you have to ask Him
And let Him make things right

So, get your cup of coffee
Or maybe have some tea
Cozy up and read a book
Then bow on bended knee

Give your heart to Jesus
Whenever you are blue
He'll glue it back together
And make it good as new

# Heaven Is About Relationships

*"Heaven is not about mansions and streets of gold, (though that is a figurative description from God's word that helps us understand its value). Heaven is actually about relationships…relationships with God and with His people"* (Paul Earnhart).

Here are **5 relationships** God in His wisdom has provided for us to get through this life.

1. **God planned for us to be born into families.**
   For most of us the family is a place where we truly belong. God gave Adam a wife as a helper (Gen. 2:20) and in marriage two actually become one in purpose (Mk. 10:8). And as we are blessed with children (Ps. 127:5), we begin learning that serving others truly IS more satisfying than serving self. The bond in the healthy family often sustains through the highs and lows of one's journey through life. We can do things of which others in the world would never forgive us, but our families give us another chance. After our children leave home, there is

a celebration whenever they return to visit. Everyone knows the story of the prodigal son (Lk. 15:11-32). Though sunk as low as one could, he was welcomed back when he decided to make changes. It is truly a blessing that God gave us a family as a place to belong.

2. **God planned for us to live in communities.** Often in Scripture we are instructed to *"'love... [our]...neighbor"* (Mk. 12:31), and *"live peaceably"* (Rom. 12:16) with those around us. Almost everyone on the earth has those who live nearby who might be inclined to help if the need should arise. When there is a disaster the first folks to show up to help are generally family and those who live nearby. What a blessing to belong to some sort of community!

3. **We are also born as a citizen of a country.** Though there are exceptions, generally, this citizenship comes with certain rights and privileges, and often even blessings that make our life here easier and more pleasant. In Acts 22:25, Paul declared his rights as a Roman citizen.

4. **We are blessed with friends.** They may come from many different areas of our lives, but we are able to share our values and experiences. Jn. 15:13 tells us a friend may even lay down his life for you!

5. **But the greatest relationship God has planned for us is provided in our spiritual family in His church.** Though aforementioned earthly relationships may not work out for us, the only relationship we really must have for a complete and satisfied life is the relationship with Christ and His children in the church, a place where we actually learn how to make ALL our relationships the best they can be. AND which will prepare us for our heavenly relationships for eternity:

*"Let everyone sweep in front of his own door, and the whole world will be clean"* (Johann Wolfgang von Goethe, 1749-1832).

Though stated over 200 years ago, this quote is still ultra-relevant today. Imagining this concept I picture families in their own abodes, taking care of their own and sweeping their own porches. What a beautiful world we would have if everyone took care of their own small place in this great big world, starting with their own family, adding their neighbors (anyone who presents a need that you can meet), their friends, and especially their spiritual family. I love that God has given us ready-made opportunities to enjoy relationships in this life and to learn to be like Him by learning to serve one another in our circles of influence. If we truly did follow this plan no one would be in need for very long! A lovely thought indeed!!

# Your Worth

I hope that you will never let
Someone else instead of you
Define yourself and who you are
For to yourself be true

You must learn to love yourself
And know what you're about
Learn to like the way you look
Both inside and the out

Don't let a man decide your fate
Don't let him bring you down
That confidence you may have lost
Can once again be found

I don't mean you should be selfish
Or think yourself too proud
But you can shine just like the sun
And dry up every cloud

Just by knowing who you are
And how you want to live
You can start to see yourself
For all that you can give

If there are things you need to fix
Get on them right away
But know that you are worth a lot
And don't forget to pray

And let the Lord define your worth
And all will turn out fine
Be humble in the sight of Him
And He will make you shine

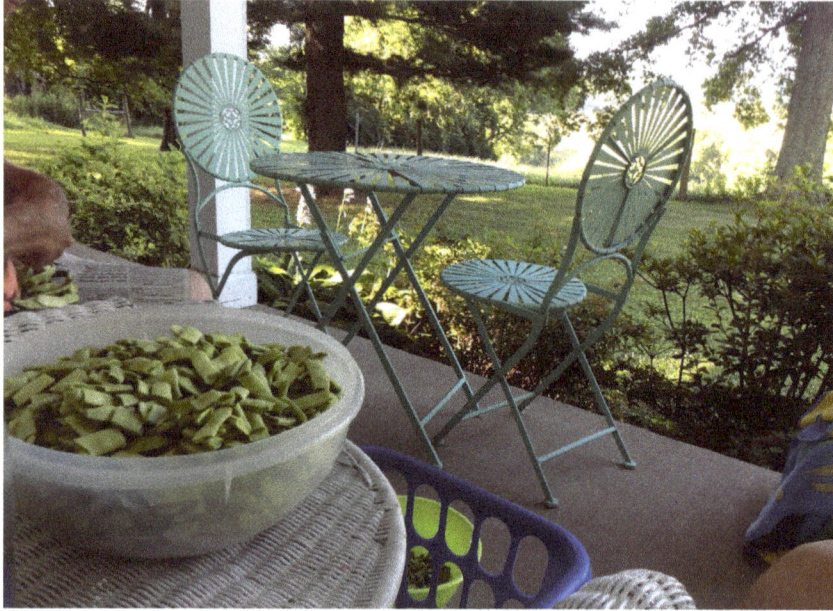

# Life's Biggest Questions

***Why Am I Here??*** *(along with the whole family of man?) Knowing how much trouble we would give God, why did he create us in the first place? Haven't we all wondered this at some point in life? It reminds me of a question every child will eventually ask his or her parents. "Mommy, why did you and daddy want to have me?" The answer to this question can bring light to our understanding of God's desire for a family His own.*

Have you ever wondered why young couples, who have freedom to go and do as they please, at some point decide they want to have a child? Have they not heard all the stories about staying up all night with a crying baby, and then having to go on to work? And have they not seen parents struggling with screaming kids at the park, or restaurant, or Walmart? Have they not calculated the expense of raising one child to adulthood, considering they may never again have an extra dollar to spend as they please? And perhaps the most frightening of all, have they not considered that this child to whom they have given their very hearts, might someday walk away and never come back? The reasons go on and on as to why a couple would choose to never have children. However, most of us, though selfish as we are, do decide to have a family. <u>Here are 3 reasons why we make that choice, and how they reflect God's reasons for desiring children and His own family.</u>

1. **We have known the benefits that come from the parent-child relationship by what we have experienced in our own families.** We have known the blessings that are afforded only from

being a cord in this close bond. And even those who may have missed out on the loving family, have perhaps watched others, and longed to share in such an experience. We look back at all that we have gone through to build that family relationship, and we laugh at the silly, crazy antics; and even appreciate the disagreements and difficult times we have shared; and we delight in recalling our happy times spent in building our life under the same roof. We want to continue in that same sweet, tangled web of life. So in a sense, these precious children are made for our own pleasure! It makes sense to assume that God wants that relationship with his children, as we are made for His good pleasure (Col.1:14). Col. 2:2 describes that idea as being *"knit together in love"* as part of the family of God (ESV). And he tells us to *"Rejoice with those who rejoice, and weep with those who weep"* (Rom. 12:15, ESV).

2. **We have a need to love and to serve!** God knew that in order for us to learn to be like Christ, and to be truly happy, we would need to learn to serve. Though I was quite selfish, when I had my first child, from that point on, I no longer thought constantly about "me." It was all about serving someone else. And in that state I learned true satisfaction. God is love. Love is at His very essence. And so He wants to share that love and make His children the beneficiaries of its blessings. He says that just like we would give our children anything we had in our power, if we thought it for their good, so is He willing to give us everything we need and ask for, if it is for our ultimate good. Luke 11:11, 13 (ESV), *"What father among you, if his son asks for a fish, will instead give him a serpent? …if you then…know how to give good gifts to your children, how much more will the heavenly Father give the Holy Spirit to those who ask him!"*

3. **We desire to have someone in our own likeness or image.** Whether we have a natural born baby or we adopt, it isn't long before others start noting the similarities they see in the child and the parents. We want our children to imitate our good qualities and we spend the years we have them teaching them to understand right from wrong. From the very beginning when God said to His Son *"Let Us make man in Our image, according to Our likeness,"* (Gen. 1:24, NASB) and on throughout the entire Scripture we learn to spend our lives becoming more like Jesus and growing into His image.

Could it be the family relationship is created by God to teach us the blessings that come from being with those who love and serve each other? And just as the children we bring into this world eventually have a choice about remaining in our family circle, so God gives us a choice to remain with Him as his obedient children, or to leave the very place where security is assured. And so, like that step of faith we take, when deciding to begin a family, and all the hope we share for a child to become a blessing to us and others in this world, God creates children, in hope that we will choose to stay with Him and be a blessing to Him and all those in His family. *"To God be the glory, great things He has done!"* (Fanny Crosby).

# A New Year

Below are five questions to ask each day to stay in-tune spiritually.

As we begin a new year, it is a good time to focus on ways to grow spiritually and become more like Christ. Asking a few simple questions each day may be a good way to stay focused and keep up a personal inventory of how we are doing. I like to ask these at the end of the day, but it is a good idea to think of them early in the morning as well...

1. **Did I fully TRUST in the Lord today?** The instructions given in God's word are for my good always, so when I made decisions, did I willingly follow His will, or are there some areas where I truly think I know what's best? Did I try and solve all my issues MY way? Or did I trust His Way, even when it seemed hard or inconvenient?

2. **Did I TALK to Him in prayer today?** Were my choices made BEFORE or AFTER laying it at His feet? Did I plunge ahead not asking for His help or advice?

3. **Did I LISTEN to Him today?** Not only did I talk to Him in prayer, but did I then search His word for answers? A good way I have discovered recently is using the YouVersion Bible App on my phone and iPad. I like to read the verse of the day in the context of the whole chapter and then personally apply it in some way to my present life and problems. I have been amazed how looking at one passage each day and internalizing and reflecting on the lessons therein, has strengthened my faith and resolve. And when

I am in a place where I don't have access to the written word, I am trying to reach into my heart where much of that word can be hidden to bring out at the appropriate time for application.

4. **Did I EXAMINE myself today?** Did I look deep into my own heart for any root of bitterness, envy, strife, or jealousy? Did I test my motives? When someone upset or disappointed me, did I look inside at self for any way I might make a difference, rather than focusing on the fault of others? Did I stop resisting temptation to treat another lower than self and remind myself giving into anger, self-pity, and complaining is giving into Satan?

5. **Did I SERVE someone else today?** As Jesus washed His disciples' feet, have I recognized and even sought out opportunity to do something (either physical or spiritual) for someone that took me out of my way or out of my comfort zone?

Let's continue in His grace and keep ourselves in tune with His will for our lives. Happy New Year!

www.ingramcontent.com/pod-product-compliance
Lightning Source LLC
Chambersburg PA
CBHW061955090426
42811CB00006B/942